GEORGE W. *Bush*

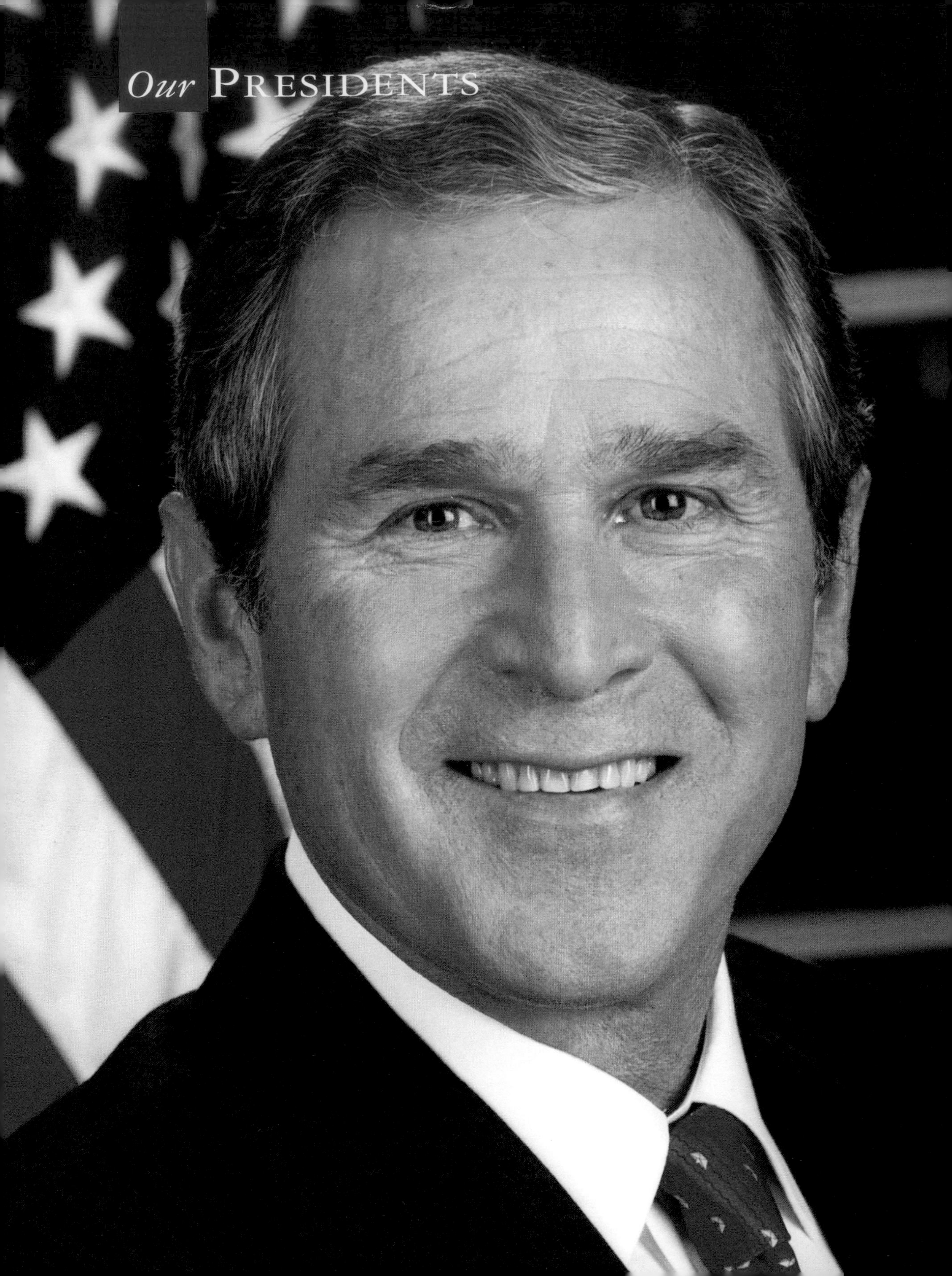

GEORGE W. Bush

By Ann Graham Gaines

SPIRIT
of America™

The Child's World®, Inc.
Chanhassen, Minnesota

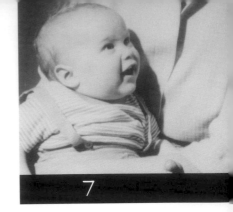

7

GEORGE W. *Bush*

Published in the United States of America by The Child's World®, Inc.
PO Box 326 • Chanhassen, MN 55317-0326 • 800-599-READ • www.childsworld.com

Acknowledgments
The Creative Spark: Mary Francis-DeMarois, Project Director; Elizabeth Sirimarco Budd, Series Editor; Robert Court, Design and Art Direction; Janine Graham, Page Layout; Jennifer Moyers, Production

The Child's World®, Inc.: Mary Berendes, Publishing Director; Katherine Stevenson, Ph. D., Revisions; Red Line Editorial, Fact Research; Cindy Klingel, Curriculum Advisor; Robert Noyed, Historical Advisor

Photos
Cover: The White House Photo Office. All interior images are courtesy of the George Bush Library (College Station, Texas) except the following: AP Photo, 36; AP Photo/Chao Soi Cheong: 35; AP Photo/Doug Mills, 37 (bottom); AP Photo/LM Otero: 28; AP Photo/POOL/Win McNamee, 37 (top); CORBIS: 13, 18, 27, 30, 32, 34; Reuters NewMedia Inc./CORBIS: 38.

Registration
The Child's World®, Inc., Spirit of America™, and their associated logos are the sole property and registered trademarks of The Child's World®, Inc.

Library of Congress Cataloging-in-Publication Data
Gaines, Ann.
    George W. Bush : our forty-third president / by Ann Graham Gaines.
        p. cm.
    Includes bibliographical references (p.   ) and index.
    ISBN 1-56766-877-1 (library bound : alk. paper)
    1. Bush, George W. (George Walker), 1946–   .—Juvenile literature. 2. Presidents—United
States—Biography—Juvenile literature. [1. Bush, George W. (George Walker), 1946– 2. Presidents.}
I. Title.
    E903 .G35 2001
    973.931'092—dc21

                                                                    2001001071

23   34   35

Contents

Chapter ONE

Growing Up

George W. Bush became the nation's 43rd president in 2001. His father had served as president a decade earlier. The two George Bushes are shown here in a photograph from 1946.

GEORGE W. BUSH BELONGS TO A FAMILY OF **politicians**, people who work as government leaders. His great-grandfather was an advisor to President Herbert Hoover. His grandfather, Prescott Bush, was a senator. His father, George Bush, was president of the United States from 1989 until 1993. George W. Bush grew up feeling proud of his family and its achievements. It seems only natural that he, too, would choose a career in **politics**.

George Walker Bush (nicknamed "George W.") was born in New Haven, Connecticut, on July 6, 1946. When George W. was born, his father, George Bush, was a student at Yale University, one of the best colleges in the country. He and George W.'s mother, Barbara, were newlyweds. They had

George W. Bush's parents, George and Barbara, both came from wealthy, successful families. The Bushes expected a great deal from their children, just as their own parents had of them. They are shown here with George W. in 1947.

met five years earlier at a country club dance. Like her husband, Barbara Bush had grown up in a rich, successful family. Her father was president of a publishing company. After George and Barbara married, she became a homemaker. George W. was the couple's first child.

George Bush excelled at Yale. He earned good grades and took part in many activities while still spending time with George W. and Barbara. By the time he graduated in 1948, he had decided to be a businessman like his father and grandfather. But George was going to try his luck with a different business: the oil industry. He accepted a job with the International Derrick and Equipment Company (IDECO) in Texas. This company sold rigs used to drill for oil. George, Barbara, and George W. moved to west Texas.

After living in cool, lush New England, it took time for the Bushes to adjust to flat, dry, dusty Texas. But it didn't take long for George Bush to succeed in the oil business. In 1948, 3,000 wells were drilled in the area where they lived. He was able to sell many rigs. In 1949, the Bushes had a second child, Pauline Robinson Bush, nicknamed "Robin." The next year, George Bush and a friend started their own company. They bought and sold **mineral** rights, which give a person or company the right to look for minerals on a piece of land. Everything was going well for the Bush family.

While George W. was growing up, his father was a leader in their home-town of Midland, Texas. He worked with a number of different community organizations, while Barbara volunteered her time to the local hospital and other groups. Both parents spent as much time as possible with their children and the rest of their family. They enjoyed spending vacations at the family summer home in Kennebunkport, Maine. When the relatives gathered, they often discussed Grandfather Prescott Bush's goal to be elected to the U.S. Senate. In 1952, he reached this goal. That same year, George W. started first grade at the local public school.

George Bush (left) hoped to achieve success in the oil industry, so he moved his young family to Texas. George W. spent most of his childhood there.

▸ George W. is the Bushes' only living child who was not born in Texas.

▸ George W.'s nickname as a child was "Junior." Today many people simply call him "W" to distinguish him from his father.

▸ George W. may not have been the best student in his class or a star athlete, but his friendly personality made him popular throughout most of his school years.

In February of 1953, the Bush family grew once again when John Ellis "Jeb" Bush was born. Just weeks later, Barbara noticed that Robin always seemed tired. She also bruised far too easily. The family doctor told the Bushes that Robin had leukemia, a rare disease that affects the **bone marrow**. Barbara Bush took Robin to a special hospital in New York. George Bush traveled back and forth between Midland and New York. In Texas, he and a partner had just started another new oil company. But when he wasn't working, he flew to New York to be with Barbara and Robin at the hospital. It was a difficult time for the entire family.

Sadly, in October of 1953, Robin died. After her death, the Bush family kept busy, which helped ease their sorrow. George continued to work hard, while Barbara took care of their family and volunteered her time. George W. participated in many activities at school and studied hard. In his free time, he loved to play Little League baseball. Over the years, the Bush family continued to grow. A third son, Neil, was born in 1955. The Bushes' fourth son, Marvin, was born a year later. In 1958, the family moved to Houston. The next year, Dorothy, the last of the Bushes' children, was born.

Interesting Facts

▸ George W. wasn't interested in politics as a child. He preferred playing baseball. "I never dreamed about being president. When I was growing up, I wanted to be Willie Mays," he has said. He spent hours playing baseball in the field behind his house and was the catcher on his Little League team.

By 1956, the Bushes had four sons. George W., age 10, is standing at far left.

In 1961, George W. enrolled at Phillips Academy, a boarding school in Andover, Massachusetts. His father had gone there when he was a boy. At Phillips, George W. played sports and was popular with the other boys. After graduating in 1964, he planned to follow in his father's footsteps once more and attend Yale University. That same year, his father set a new example for his son to follow. He began his political career, running for election to the Senate.

George W. (shown here with his parents) followed in his father's footsteps from the start. He attended the same high school and then graduated from Yale University. He used his father's success as an example to follow.

LIFE IN TEXAS CHANGED FOREVER ON JANUARY 10, 1901. ON THAT DAY, A work crew drilling for oil found one of the biggest gushers of all time at Spindletop, shown here. People had known for years that there was oil underground in Texas. In the 1880s, many began to drill, hoping to find a big deposit and become rich. After Spindletop, an oil boom took place. "Wildcatters" found rich oil fields in the state's panhandle area and in western Texas. By the time George Bush arrived in Texas, the oil business was well established. But there was still plenty of oil to be found. A second boom earned a fortune for Bush and many other people in Odessa and Midland. Working in the oil business became another family tradition. George W. opened an oil company in 1978 and would work in the industry throughout the 1980s.

Chapter TWO

Out into the World

George W. attended Yale University from 1964 through 1968.

IN 1964, GEORGE W. BUSH GRADUATED from high school. He spent his summer vacation home in Texas, helping with his father's Senate **campaign**. George W. went to political meetings, gave speeches, and talked to voters. In the fall, he left for Connecticut to begin college at Yale University.

George W. found his classes at Yale much more difficult than those in high school. He was never an outstanding student at Yale, but he enjoyed himself. As soon as he arrived, he got to know as many people as he could. Soon he knew almost every student. Some of these new friends would remain close to George W. long after he left college. A few even worked as his advisors when he became a politician. At Yale, George W. played baseball and rugby. He also served on the Social Council, which planned student activities such as dances and parties.

While at Yale, George W. was always reminded of his father, who had been an excellent student and athlete nearly 20 years earlier. George Bush's name appeared on trophies and plaques all over campus. In addition, during George W.'s first year, the school newspaper covered his father's race for the Senate. George W. never talked with his friends about his father's campaign, but he did go home to Texas in time for the election. His father lost, but soon began making plans for future elections.

George W. enjoyed his social life at Yale. He met people who would become lifelong friends.

When George W.'s first year at Yale ended, he took a summer job working for an oil company in Louisiana. In his second year of college, he joined a fraternity, a club of male students who spent their free time together. George W. and his friends liked to have fun when they weren't too busy with their studies. They enjoyed playing sports, giving parties, and meeting new people. The following summer, George W.'s father was running for the U.S. House of Representatives. George W. returned to Texas to work on the campaign.

Back at Yale that fall, George W. was elected president of his fraternity. Friends admired his leadership ability. But at that time, fraternities held little appeal for most of Yale's students. Many students thought these clubs were too traditional and old-fashioned. George W. began to feel out of place, especially after his father won the election in November.

George Bush was a member of the Republican Party, one of the nation's two most powerful **political parties**. Most Republicans are conservative, meaning they want things to stay the same. Many students believed Republicans did not want to help the poor or give equal rights to minorities. Like young people all over the country, many Yale students wanted the nation to change. George W. thought differently. Like his father, he was more conservative.

George W. finished college in 1968, a year of great turmoil in the United States. The nation was sending thousands of soldiers to fight in the Vietnam War. This war was fought in Asia between the countries of North Vietnam and South Vietnam. The U.S. joined the war on the side of South Vietnam. Many Americans did not think the U.S. should be involved in the war. College students began to hold **protests**. They did not want any more Americans sent to Vietnam, where thousands had died in battle.

At the same time, the Civil Rights Movement was going strong. African Americans were struggling for equal rights and better treatment. Their peaceful protests were often met with violence. When civil rights leader Martin Luther King, Jr. was **assassinated** in April, the situation grew even more tense and the protests more violent. During this difficult time, George W. was interested in his friendships

The 1960s were a time of difficult change in the United States. Many college students protested U.S. involvement in the Vietnam War. Civil rights demonstrations sometimes turned violent. But in these difficult times, George W.'s interest in politics had not yet blossomed.

and his schoolwork, not in changing the world. His friends later remembered that he never liked to talk about politics in those days. He did not protest against the war or join the fight for civil rights. He preferred to concentrate on finishing college.

Even though George W. went to school in New England for several years, he always considered himself a Texan. After graduating from Yale in 1968, he was happy to return home. He joined the Texas Air National Guard, a military **reserve** group. In November, the guard sent him to an air force base in Georgia to learn to fly military airplanes. By December of the next year, he had completed his training and returned to Texas. There he reported to Ellington Air Force Base near Houston every weekend. During the week, George W. worked for a company that operated large farms. He also took part in another political campaign for his father. He realized that he enjoyed life on the campaign trail.

By this time, George W. was thinking about entering politics himself. He considered running for a seat in the Texas State Senate but decided he was not ready. Instead, he finished

George W. was a pilot in the Texas Air National Guard from 1968 until 1973. He attended flight school and flew F-102s.

his time in the National Guard and enrolled at Harvard University's business school. After graduating with a **master's degree** in 1975, he headed back to Texas. He immediately went to work in the oil business. There he worked as a "land man," learning who owned the mineral rights to a property and then leasing or buying them.

In 1977, George W. Bush announced that he would run for Congress the following year. He also started to date Laura Welch, an elementary-school librarian. The couple soon fell in love and married on November 5. They spent the next year campaigning. When Election Day arrived, George W. lost the race, but he had plenty to keep him busy. That same year, he had started his own oil company. He became part-owner of a number of oil wells and hoped to strike it rich. Friends and

Like his father, George W. decided to seek his fortune in the oil business. He is shown here (at left in the photograph) talking with an oil-field worker.

family members hoped he would succeed and invested money in his business.

George W. continued to work in the oil industry throughout the 1980s. He also spent a great deal of time working on his father's political campaigns. All the while, he still planned to run in another election one day.

George W. married Laura Welch just three months after they met in 1977. He once said the best decision he ever made was asking Laura to marry him. "I'm not sure the best decision she ever made was saying yes," he joked, "but fortunately, she did."

IN THE 1960S, THE AMERICAN ARMY **DRAFTED** MANY YOUNG MEN AND SENT them to fight in Vietnam. Thousands of American soldiers died there. The war became a matter of conflict in the United States. Many young people did not want to fight. College students received deferments, which meant they did not have to join the military as long as they remained in school. When Bush and his Yale classmates graduated, they would be drafted and sent to Vietnam unless they served their country in another way.

George W. joined the Texas Air National Guard, a reserve corps. Soldiers in the reserves did not usually go to Vietnam, and this was a relief for the Bush family. But George W. wanted to serve. His father had been a pilot in World War II and almost died when his plane was shot down. Fortunately, a submarine crew rescued him. When George W. met with the commander of the National Guard, he said he wanted to join because he hoped to be a fighter pilot, just as his dad had been.

Chapter THREE

Governor of Texas

When Ronald Reagan (left) was elected president in 1980, George Bush (right) was elected vice president. George W. had worked on the exciting campaign and was thrilled when his father won.

IN 1980, GEORGE W. BUSH WORKED FOR THE Republican presidential campaign, and his father was elected vice president. Ronald Reagan was elected president. In 1981, George W.'s wife, Laura, gave birth to twins. Vice President and Mrs. Bush enjoyed showing off their grandchildren to friends in Washington, D.C.

George Bush was vice president for eight years. In 1988, he became the Republican **candidate** for president. George W. worked hard for his father's campaign, talking to reporters and traveling around the country. He gave speeches and won votes for his father. When George Bush won the election, George W. helped his father prepare to become president.

24

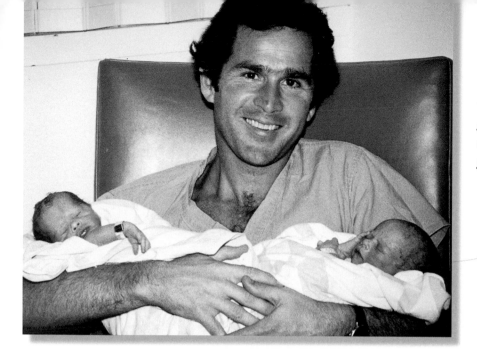

The Bushes' twin daughters were born in 1981. The girls were named Barbara and Jenna, after their grandmothers.

After his father's **inauguration**, George W. went back to Texas. He and Laura bought a new house in Dallas, where George W. had become part-owner of the Texas Rangers baseball team. Bush helped manage the team's business matters. He went to their games and enjoyed hanging out with the players in the dugout and locker room. Although George W. loved working with the Rangers, his dream of entering politics had not disappeared. He began to plan for the future, hoping to find the right time to enter a political race.

George W. was becoming famous all over Texas, both because his father was president and because of the Texas Rangers. In 1992, he helped his father run for president once

25

again. That year, however, Democrat Bill Clinton beat President Bush in the election. (The Democrats are the other major U.S. political party.)

While he was campaigning for his father, George W. began preparing for a campaign of his own. Ann Richards had been elected governor of Texas in 1990. A grandmother, Richards had begun her political career when she was already in middle age. Richards was an outspoken, funny woman who loved to tell stories. She became well known after she delivered a speech at the Democratic Party's national convention in 1988.

Texans approved of the job Richards did in office. Nevertheless, George W. Bush thought he could win the 1994 election. Throughout his campaign, he talked about several key issues, including the need to change certain laws. He also wanted to see improvements in education and a drop in crime. Finally, he wanted to change the **welfare** system. He believed that people should be helped to find work to support themselves, rather than receiving government money for long periods of time.

Richards said she did not believe that George W. would be able to bring about those changes. For one thing, he did not have experience in government. In response, George W. told Texans they should vote for him because he was new to politics. He promised to bring fresh ideas to the governorship. To the surprise of many Texans, George W. Bush won the election. Looking back, many people said Richards talked too much about Bush and not enough about what she wanted to do for Texas.

As governor, Bush set right to work to make his campaign promises come true. He

George W. Bush ran against Governor Ann Richards (left) in the 1994 election for governor of Texas. Many people thought Richards couldn't lose the election. But when the votes were counted, Bush had won.

convinced politicians to change certain Texas laws. One of these changes made it more difficult for people to file "frivolous lawsuits." This meant people could not take others to court without a good reason.

With encouragement and advice from his wife, Governor Bush pushed to improve the state's schools. He pressured teachers to work harder and improve their students' test scores. Bush then gained nation-wide attention for enforcing the state's death penalty. When prisoners receive the death penalty, they are put to death as punishment for their crimes. Many people respected Bush's support of the death penalty, but others believed it was wrong.

As governor of Texas, Bush worked hard to keep the promises he made during his campaign. This photo shows Bush after speaking at the 1998 Greater Dallas Chamber of Commerce luncheon in Dallas.

George W. Bush continues to be close to his parents and his sister and brothers. Everyone in the family chipped in to help him campaign for the 2000 presidential election. The Bushes' extended family is shown here at their vacation home in Maine.

Governor Bush also worked to reform the state's welfare system. If needy Texans received money from the government, they had to look for a job or learn skills to help them find work. Otherwise, the government would stop supporting them. Many Texans liked what Governor Bush did in office.

Texas held its next election for governor, and Bush ran for a second **term**. Throughout his first term, he had gained increasing support from the people of Texas. His opponent in 1998 was Garry Mauro, who was not well known. Bush had a good chance of winning the election.

Some people said Bush should not be reelected because he might run for president in 2000. If he ran for president, he would have to campaign all over the country instead

As the 2000 election approached, George W. Bush announced his plans to enter the race for the presidency, once again following in his father's successful footsteps.

of spending time on his duties as governor. Bush refused to talk about the possibility. His staff said that he was thinking about the 1998 election for governor, not the 2000 election for president. In November, Bush won by a large number of votes.

As many predicted, Governor Bush soon announced that he was a Republican candidate for president. When Bush started this new campaign, he was one of several candidates. At first, it seemed as if he might not win the Republicans' **nomination**. Critics pointed out that he had little experience in government. But Bush and his supporters quickly raised a great deal of money and continued their campaign. In the summer of 2000, George W. Bush won the Republican nomination.

GEORGE W. BUSH HAS DESCRIBED his wife, Laura, as "one of the great listeners. . . . And since I'm one of the big talkers, it was a great fit."

Laura Welch was born on November 4, 1946, in Midland, Texas. When she was in second grade, she told her father, who owned a construction company, that she wanted to be a teacher when she grew up. This would remain her dream. A smart, quiet girl, Laura attended Southern Methodist University after she graduated from high school. She earned a degree in education and became a math teacher.

After a few years, Laura realized that she was not happy teaching math, but she did like reading to her class. So she enrolled at the University of Texas, where she earned a master's degree in library science. When she graduated, she found a position as a school librarian.

In 1977, friends invited Laura to dinner to meet George W., who was preparing to run for Congress. Before they met, Laura assumed she would not like George W. because she was not interested in politics. She liked him at once, however, and especially admired his sense of humor. Laura and George W. married within months of their meeting. After their marriage, Laura never worked, although she often volunteered her time to help others. When George W. became governor of Texas, she encouraged him to work to improve the state's educational system. She worked with programs that promoted reading. The people of Texas often saw Laura Bush at story hours, reading aloud to children.

During George W.'s campaign for the presidency, Laura admitted that she did not look forward to leading her life in the public eye. But she supported her husband because she thought he would make an excellent president.

Chapter FOUR

The New President

Bush entered the 2000 presidential election with a great deal of support from the Republican Party. To win votes from more Americans, he promised to be a "compassionate conservative." This meant that he would not change the country in drastic ways, and that he would help people in need.

WHILE RUNNING FOR PRESIDENT, George W. Bush described himself as a "**compassionate** conservative." In earlier elections, Republicans often talked about building the military, fighting crime, and strengthening the **economy**. Bush said that besides doing those things, he wanted to improve education, health care, and assistance to the elderly. Bush also promised to encourage cooperation between the government's Republicans and Democrats, who had rarely been in agreement in recent years.

When the campaign began, some people thought Bush's opponent, Vice President Al Gore, might win. Even though President Bill Clinton had been **impeached** during his second term, most Americans approved of the job he and Gore had done in their two terms. They liked the fact that the economy had been strong. Most Americans had jobs and earned good livings.

As the 2000 campaign went on, it was clear that the November 7 election would be close—but it was even closer than expected. In Florida, the two candidates were almost tied. Reporters announced first that Gore had won and then that Bush had won. By the end of the night, no one really knew who the winner was. Democrats and Republicans began to disagree about how the Florida votes had been counted. In some areas, the votes were counted again. Finally, more than a month after the election, the U.S. **Supreme Court** stopped the recounting. George W. Bush was declared the winner on December 13, 2000.

Bush had little time to prepare to take office. He quickly hired his staff and announced who he wanted in his cabinet, his group of close advisors. On January 20, 2001, George W. Bush became the 43rd president of the United States. Many people watched the inaugural celebrations. Soon afterward, Bush met with both Democratic and Republican leaders to discuss what he hoped to accomplish.

Interesting Facts

▶ The Republican Party chose Dick Cheney as Bush's vice-presidential candidate. Cheney had served as secretary of defense when Bush's father was president. Many people believed Cheney's experience made Bush a stronger candidate.

▶ The close election of 2000 created ill will among Americans. After George W. Bush was finally declared the winner, he talked about his desire to help mend the divisions that had arisen in the country. He promised that he and Vice President Dick Cheney were "bringing America together."

Early in Bush's term, the members of his cabinet were approved by the Senate and sworn into office. With his cabinet in place, President Bush set to work to fulfill his campaign promises, including pushing for a large tax cut. There were problems to face, but the nation was at peace and doing well.

Less than nine months later, Bush was faced with one of the worst crises any president has ever confronted. On September 11, **terrorists hijacked** three enormous airliners. They flew the planes into the busy World Trade Center in New York City and into the Pentagon, the nation's military headquarters in Washington, D. C. The two World Trade Center towers were completely destroyed, and part of the Pentagon was badly damaged. A fourth hijacked plane crashed in Pennsylvania without reaching its target, apparently because its passengers fought back.

The planes had been hijacked shortly after takeoff and were full of highly explosive jet fuel. The World Trade Center towers were well built, but they could not withstand the extreme heat of the burning fuel. The upper floors collapsed and fell, causing the lower floors to collapse as well. People still trying to escape the buildings

George W. Bush became the 43rd president on January 20, 2001. Within days, he began to set his plans in motion.

were killed, as were firefighters and police officers trying to help them.

The attacks, which killed over 3,000 innocent people, shocked the nation and the world. And because they were so unexpected and took place so quickly, no one knew what else might happen. Were more attacks planned? What other targets might be hit? Was the president himself in danger?

As the nation and the world struggled to come to grips with what had happened, Bush vowed to find and punish those responsible. Evidence pointed to Osama bin Laden, a wealthy Saudi Arabian who was believed to be the leader of a group called Al-Qaida. Al-Qaida's members had a deep hatred for Western nations, especially the United States, and had been connected to other terrorist activities.

Bin Laden and Al-Qaida were based in Afghanistan. This rugged country was under the control of the Taliban, a political and religious group with views similar to Bin Laden's. Under

The events of September 11, 2001 will never be forgotten. Here you can see the explosion from the second plane as it hit the second tower in New York.

Interesting Facts

▶ President Bush urged Americans to be cautious after the attacks, but to resume their normal lives. At Game 3 of the 2001 World Series, Bush walked out alone before a huge crowd to throw the opening pitch.

Osama Bin Laden is shown speaking at a 1998 meeting in Afghanistan.

Interesting Facts

▶ Shortly after the attacks, Americans faced a new fear. Several letters carrying a deadly disease called **anthrax** were mailed to politicians and news organizations. Some people who came in contact with the letters became ill or even died. At first it was thought that the Al-Qaida terrorists might be attacking the nation through "biological warfare." But no connection with the terrorists was found.

the Taliban's harsh rule, music, movies, and many other forms of expression were forbidden. Taliban rule was especially brutal to women. Afghan women could no longer work or go to school, seek proper medical care, or even go outside of their homes alone. Those who broke the Taliban's rules were severely punished.

As more evidence about the attacks came in, the United States announced a war on terrorism and began to attack Taliban strongholds in Afghanistan. Armed forces of the United States and its allies worked with Afghan leaders and soldiers who wanted to rid their nation of Taliban rule. The combined forces did end the Taliban's rule, capturing or killing many of its leaders and soldiers. The hunt was still on, however, for the remaining Al-Qaida leaders, including Osama bin Laden. By March of 2002, no one knew whether Bin Laden was still alive, and if so, where he was hiding.

The American people strongly supported how the president handled the attacks and their aftermath. The disagreements over who had won the presidential election seemed far away. Yet new concerns and disagreements were appearing, too. The American economy was still slow, and the nation's leaders had sharply different views on how

to encourage its growth. President Bush proposed a budget that would spend more on fighting terrorism and defending the homeland while still cutting taxes. This would mean the government would be running a deficit, spending more money than it made. Bush also proposed spending **Social Security** money that was already set aside to make payments to retired taxpayers. Many leaders disagreed with Bush's proposal.

As U.S. troops and warplanes moved into position, President Bush addressed Congress on September 20, 2001. He told Americans to prepare for a long war against terrorism.

Another problem was the collapse of the nation's seventh-largest company, an oil company called Enron. When Enron suddenly declared **bankruptcy**, thousands of people lost the money they had invested. Congress began major investigations into Enron's activities. Concerns were raised over the president's and vice president's dealings with Enron. Enron had given a great deal of money to the election campaigns of the president and many other politicians.

The president walked through the honor guard as he prepared to address more than 1,000 people gathered at the White House on March 11, 2002. The day marked the six-month anniversary of the terrorist attacks on America.

George W. Bush's first year in office was a challenging and difficult one, yet he remained eager to pursue his vision for the American nation and its people. And the American people, reminded of the value of their freedom by the terrorist attacks, were still offering him their support in the new year.

WHEN THE TERRORIST ATTACKS OF
September 11 began, President Bush
was in Florida, getting ready to meet
with a class of second-graders. An
adviser told him that a plane had just
hit one of the World Trade Center
towers, but that the crash was thought
to be an accident. Bush was in the
classroom when his chief of staff whis-
pered, "A second plane hit the second
tower. America is under attack." Bush
talked briefly with the class, and then
excused himself. He had work to do.

Vice President Cheney was at the White House when the attacks took place.
When radar showed a plane headed toward the building, Secret Service agents took
Cheney downstairs to a protected underground bunker. The plane ended up
changing direction and crashing into the Pentagon building. Defense Secretary
Donald Rumsfeld was in the Pentagon when the plane hit. He rushed to help
with the rescue work until he was urged to move to a safer location.

Events moved quickly in the next few hours. The president had planned to
fly straight back to Washington on his official plane, Air Force One. But rumors of
threats to Air Force One sent the president first to Louisiana and then to Nebraska.
Bush was impatient to return to Washington despite any danger. "The American
people want to know where their president is," he told a Secret Service agent.

By that evening, Bush was back in Washington. After addressing an anxious
nation on television, he met with Cheney and other advisors to plan a response to
the attacks. Bush wrote in his diary about that day, "We cannot allow a terrorist
thug to hold us hostage. My hope is that this will provide an opportunity for us to
rally the world against terrorism."

1946 George Walker Bush is born on July 6 in New Haven, Connecticut. His parents are George and Barbara Bush.

1968 After graduating from college (Yale University), Bush joins the Texas Air National Guard and goes to flight school to become a pilot.

1973 Bush enrolls in business school at Harvard University.

1975 Bush earns his master's degree from Harvard University. He goes into the oil business.

1977 Bush announces he will run for election to Congress in 1978. He meets a school librarian named Laura Welch, whom he marries in November.

1978 Bush loses the election for Congress.

1980 George Bush, father of George W. Bush, is elected vice president of the United States. Ronald Reagan is elected president.

1988 George W. Bush works on his father's successful campaign for the presidency. George W. becomes one of the owners of the Texas Rangers baseball team.

1994 Bush runs in the election for governor of Texas. He defeats his opponent, Ann Richards, even though she has been a popular governor for the past four years.

1995 Early in his term, Bush becomes well known across the country when his enforcement of Texas's death penalty receives criticism. Many of his acts as governor are well received, however, and he begins to gain respect from the people of Texas.

1998 Bush is reelected governor of Texas. Many Texans believe he will soon become a candidate for the 2000 presidential election.

1999 After declaring himself a candidate for the 2000 presidential election, Bush spends time traveling around the country, trying to gather support for his campaign. He and his supporters raise $37 million to pay for his campaign, more than any other candidate in history.

2000 In July, the Republican Party nominates George W. Bush as its candidate for president. The Democratic Party nominates Vice President Al Gore as its candidate. The election is extremely close, and throughout the fall, Americans wonder who the next president will be. On Election Day, no winner is declared because the vote is so close in Florida. The Democratic Party asks that many of Florida's votes be recounted. After 36 days, the U.S. Supreme Court decides that the recounts must stop. George W. Bush is declared president in December.

2001 George W. Bush is inaugurated on January 20. After taking office, he works for a tax cut that he believes will help the struggling economy. On September 11, terrorists fly hijacked airliners into New York's World Trade Center as well as the Pentagon, the nation's military headquarters in Washington, D.C. Evidence points to Osama bin Laden, whose Al-Qaida terrorist network has been operating out of Afghanistan. The United States and its allies begin a war on terrorism, attacking suspected Al-Qaida hideouts and the strongholds of Afghanistan's Taliban government. The Taliban government is ousted, but Bin Laden and some of Al-Qaida's other leaders cannot be found.

2002 President Bush pledges to continue the war on terrorism and to defend the homeland. He proposes a budget that would increase military spending and cut taxes. Critics object to Bush's proposal because it relies on deficit spending and borrowing from money set aside for Social Security. Bush also faces problems associated with the collapse of Enron, an oil company that had donated heavily to his and other politicians' election campaigns. Despite a sluggish economy and other concerns, public support for Bush remains high.

anthrax (AN-thraks)
Anthrax is a disease caused by bacteria. Several letters containing anthrax were mailed to different people following the September 11, 2001 attacks.

assassinated (uh-SASS-ih-nay-ted)
Assassinate means to murder someone, especially a well-known person. Martin Luther King, Jr. was assassinated in 1968.

bone marrow (BOHN MAIR-roh)
Bone marrow is the soft matter found inside bones, where blood cells are created. Leukemia is a disease that affects bone marrow.

campaign (kam-PAYN)
A campaign is the process of running in an election, including activities such as giving speeches or attending rallies. George W. Bush worked on many of his father's political campaigns.

candidate (KAN-dih-det)
A candidate is a person running in an election. George W. Bush was the Republican candidate for president in 2000.

compassionate (kum-PASH-eh-nit)
People who are compassionate want to help people in need. During the election of 2000, George W. Bush said he was a "compassionate conservative."

drafted (DRAF-ted)
When people are drafted, they are required by law to join the military. During the Vietnam War, thousands of young American men were drafted into the military.

economy (ee-KON-uh-mee)
An economy is the way money is earned and spent. George W. Bush wanted to help the U.S. economy.

hijacked (HY-jakt)
When a vehicle has been hijacked, someone has illegally and forcefully taken control of it. On September 11, 2001, four American airliners were hijacked by terrorists.

impeached (im-PEECHD)
If the House of Representatives votes to impeach, it charges the president with a crime or serious misdeed. President Bill Clinton was impeached in 1998.

inauguration (ih-nawg-yuh-RAY-shun)
An inauguration is the ceremony that takes place when a new leader begins a term. George W. Bush's inauguration took place on January 20, 2001.

master's degree (MAS-terz deh-GREE)
A master's degree is an advanced degree earned after graduating from college. George W. Bush earned a master's degree at Harvard Business School.

mineral (MIN-er-el)
A mineral is a substance obtained by mining, digging, or drilling in the earth. Coal, gold, and oil are all minerals.

nomination (nom-ih-NAY-shun)
If someone receives a nomination, he or she is chosen by a political party to run for an office. George W. Bush received the Republican presidential nomination in 2000.

**political parties
(puh-LIT-ih-kul PAR-teez)**
Political parties are groups of people who
share similar ideas about how to run a government. The two major political parties in the
United States are the Democratic Party and
the Republican Party.

politicians (pawl-ih-TISH-anz)
Politicians are people who hold offices in
government. Many people in the Bush family
are, or once were, politicians.

politics (PAWL-ih-tiks)
Politics refers to the actions and practices of
the government. The Bush family has been
very active in politics.

protests (PROH-tests)
Protests are public statements or gatherings
where people speak out to say something is
wrong. During the Vietnam War, many
Americans attended protests to speak out
against the war.

reserve (ree-ZERV)
A reserve is part of a country's military that is
not on active duty, but is on call in case of
emergency. Members of the reserves receive
military training. They report for duty on
weekends or for a few weeks a year.

**Social Security
(SOH-shull seh-KYUR-ih-tee)**
Social Security is a government program that
pays people who are retired, unemployed, or
disabled. To help the economy, President Bush
proposed spending Social Security money.

Supreme Court (suh-PREEM KORT)
The U.S. Supreme Court is the highest court
in the United States. The Supreme Court
declared in December of 2000 that there
would be no further recounts in Florida in
the 2000 presidential election.

term (TERM)
A term is the length of time a politician can
keep his or her position by law. George W.
Bush was the first Texas governor elected to
two consecutive four-year terms.

terrorists (TEHR-ur-ists)
Terrorists are people who use violence and
fear to try to force others to do what they
want. The people who carried out the
September 11, 2001, attacks on New York
and Washington were terrorists.

welfare (WELL-fair)
Welfare is aid provided by the government to
poor or needy people. As governor of Texas,
George W. Bush planned to improve the
state's welfare system.

Our PRESIDENTS

President	Birthplace	Life Dates	Term	Political Party	First Lady
George Washington	Virginia	1732–1799	1789–1797	None	Martha Dandridge Custis Washington
John Adams	Massachusetts	1735–1826	1797–1801	Federalist	Abigail Smith Adams
Thomas Jefferson	Virginia	1743–1826	1801–1809	Democratic-Republican	widower
James Madison	Virginia	1751–1836	1809–1817	Democratic-Republican	Dolley Payne Todd Madison
James Monroe	Virginia	1758–1831	1817–1825	Democratic-Republican	Elizabeth "Eliza" Kortright Monroe
John Quincy Adams	Massachusetts	1767–1848	1825–1829	Democratic-Republican	Louisa Catherine Johnson Adams
Andrew Jackson	South Carolina	1767–1845	1829–1837	Democrat	widower
Martin Van Buren	New York	1782–1862	1837–1841	Democrat	widower
William Henry Harrison	Virginia	1773–1841	1841	Whig	Anna Tuthill Symmes Harrison
John Tyler	Virginia	1790–1862	1841–1845	Whig	Letitia Christian Tyler Julia Gardiner Tyler
James Polk	North Carolina	1795–1849	1845–1849	Democrat	Sarah Childress Polk

Our PRESIDENTS

President	Birthplace	Life Dates	Term	Political Party	First Lady
Zachary Taylor	Virginia	1784–1850	1849–1850	Whig	Margaret Mackall Smith Taylor
Millard Fillmore	New York	1800–1874	1850–1853	Whig	Abigail Powers Fillmore
Franklin Pierce	New Hampshire	1804–1869	1853–1857	Democrat	Jane Means Appleton Pierce
James Buchanan	Pennsylvania	1791–1868	1857–1861	Democrat	never married
Abraham Lincoln	Kentucky	1809–1865	1861–1865	Republican	Mary Todd Lincoln
Andrew Johnson	North Carolina	1808–1875	1865–1869	Democrat	Eliza McCardle Johnson
Ulysses S. Grant	Ohio	1822–1885	1869–1877	Republican	Julia Dent Grant
Rutherford B. Hayes	Ohio	1822–1893	1877–1881	Republican	Lucy Ware Webb Hayes
James A. Garfield	Ohio	1831–1881	1881	Republican	Lucretia Rudolph Garfield
Chester A. Arthur	Vermont	1829–1886	1881–1885	Republican	widower
Grover Cleveland	New Jersey	1837–1908	1885–1889	Democrat	Frances Folsom Cleveland

Our PRESIDENTS

	President	Birthplace	Life Dates	Term	Political Party	First Lady
	Benjamin Harrison	Ohio	1833–1901	1889–1893	Republican	Caroline Lavina Scott Harrison
	Grover Cleveland	New Jersey	1837–1908	1893–1897	Democrat	Frances Folsom Cleveland
	William McKinley	Ohio	1843–1901	1897–1901	Republican	Ida Saxton McKinley
	Theodore Roosevelt	New York	1858–1919	1901–1909	Republican	Edith Kermit Carow Roosevelt
	William Howard Taft	Ohio	1857–1930	1909–1913	Republican	Helen Herron Taft
	Woodrow Wilson	Virginia	1856–1924	1913–1921	Democrat	Ellen L. Axson Wilson / Edith Bolling Galt Wilson
	Warren G. Harding	Ohio	1865–1923	1921–1923	Republican	Florence Kling De Wolfe Harding
	Calvin Coolidge	Vermont	1872–1933	1923–1929	Republican	Grace Anna Goodhue Coolidge
	Herbert Hoover	Iowa	1874–1964	1929–1933	Republican	Lou Henry Hoover
	Franklin D. Roosevelt	New York	1882–1945	1933–1945	Democrat	Anna Eleanor Roosevelt Roosevelt
	Harry S. Truman	Missouri	1884–1972	1945–1953	Democrat	Elizabeth "Bess" Virginia Wallace Truman

Our PRESIDENTS

President	Birthplace	Life Dates	Term	Political Party	First Lady
Dwight D. Eisenhower	Texas	1890–1969	1953–1961	Republican	Mamie Geneva Doud Eisenhower
John F. Kennedy	Massachusetts	1917–1963	1961–1963	Democrat	Jacqueline Lee Bouvier Kennedy
Lyndon Baines Johnson	Texas	1908–1973	1963–1969	Democrat	Claudia "Lady Bird" Alta Taylor Johnson
Richard M. Nixon	California	1913 1994	1969–1974	Republican	Thelma "Pat" Catherine Patricia Ryan Nixon
Gerald R. Ford	Nebraska	1913–	1974–1977	Republican	Elizabeth "Betty" Bloomer Warren Ford
James Earl Carter	Georgia	1924–	1977–1981	Democrat	Rosalynn Smith Carter
Ronald Reagan	Illinois	1911–	1981–1989	Republican	Nancy Davis Reagan
George Bush	Massachusetts	1924–	1989–1993	Republican	Barbara Pierce Bush
William J. Clinton	Arkansas	1946–	1993–2001	Democrat	Hillary Rodham Clinton
George W. Bush	Connecticut	1946–	2001–	Republican	Laura Welch Bush

Presidential FACTS

Qualifications

To run for president, a candidate must
- be at least 35 years old
- be a citizen who was born in the United States
- have lived in the United States for 14 years

Term of Office

A president's term of office is four years. No president can stay in office for more than two terms.

Election Date

The presidential election takes place every four years on the first Tuesday of November.

Inauguration Date

Presidents are inaugurated on January 20.

Oath of Office

I do solemnly swear I will faithfully execute the office of the President of the United States and will to the best of my ability preserve, protect, and defend the Constitution of the United States.

Write a Letter to the President

One of the best things about being a U.S. citizen is that Americans get to participate in their government. They can speak out if they feel government leaders aren't doing their jobs. They can also praise leaders who are going the extra mile. Do you have something you'd like the president to do? Should the president worry more about the environment and encourage people to recycle? Should the government spend more money on our schools? You can write a letter to the president to say how you feel!

1600 Pennsylvania Avenue
Washington, D.C. 20500

You can even send an e-mail to: president@whitehouse.gov

46

For Further INFORMATION

Internet Sites

Visit a children's site about George W. Bush:
http://www.georgewbush.com/youth/

Read a biography on George W. Bush:
http://www.infoplease.com/ipa/A0878291.html

Learn more about George W. Bush:
http://www.georgewbush.com/

Visit a page about George W. Bush on the CNN network's Web site:
http://www.cnn.com/SPECIALS/2000/democracy/bush/stories/bush/

Learn more about the Bush family at the George Bush Presidential Library site:
http://www.csdl.tamu.edu/bushlib/

View a time line of what happened after the election of 2000:
http://cbc.ca/news/indepth/facts/recount_timeline.html

Learn more about the attacks on September 11, 2001:
http://www.cnn.com/SPECIALS/2001/trade.center/

Learn more about all the presidents and visit the White House:
http://www.whitehouse.gov/WH/glimpse/presidents/html/presidents.html
http://www.thepresidency.org/presinfo.htm
http://www.americanpresidents.org/

Books

Aaseng, Nathan. *Business Builders in Oil.* Minneapolis: Oliver Press, 2000.

Francis, Sandra. *George Bush: Our Forty-First President.* Chanhassen, MN: The Child's World, 2002.

Gaines, Ann Graham. *William J. Clinton: Our Forty-Second President.* Chanhassen, MN: The Child's World, 2002.

Galt, Margot Fortunato. *Stop This War: Americans Protest of the Conflict in Vietnam.* Minneapolis: Lerner, 2000.

Heiss, Arlene McGrath. *Barbara Bush.* Philadelphia: Chelsea House, 1992.

Index